MW00422609

The Life Impact Story

A Safe Place to Go . . .

A Caring Person to Talk to . . .

MICHAEL BEESON

Thanks for being with us on this journey!
Dave & Sheri
I Cor 15:58

The Life Impact Story, Copyright © 2015 Life Impact, Inc.

All rights reserved.

(www.LifeImpactMinistries.net)

Scripture taken from The Holy Bible, New International Version®
(NIV®), Copyright ©1973, 1978, 1984 by International Bible Society. All
rights reserved worldwide.

ISBN-13: 978-1514118467
ISBN-10: 1514118467

DEDICATION

The LI Story is dedicated to our Donor Team!

Without YOU this work would not have started,
and without YOU hundreds of Christian workers
would not have received personal care.

Because of YOU,
Kingdom workers have been strengthened globally
for Kingdom impact!

Thanks for joining with Life Impact staff in this strategic venture.

CONTENTS

INTRODUCTION:
Why Does Life Impact Exist?

The number of people in Christian ministry leaving their vocations as pastors and missionaries substantially exceeds the replacement rate. This is challenging work, and those who do it can come to feel overwhelmed by the workload and, in more and more cases, by the hostile environments they work in.

Dave and Sheri Grissen have devoted their lives to Christian ministry, much of it overseas in countries where they faced difficult circumstances. These experiences led them, after returning to the U.S.A. from a 28-year missions career, to create places for pastors and missionaries to take time out in a safe, supportive, and sometimes therapeutic environment. They created . . . a SAFE PLACE for Christian workers to go . . . and provided a CARING PERSON for these workers to talk to.

The Grissens established the first such retreat in 2003 in their home in Sunriver, Oregon and named it "The Sunriver Oasis." Soon it was booked often, and in 2006 the Lord began sending them other people with appropriate backgrounds to establish similar places elsewhere.

As of this writing there are twelve Oases around the world. What follows are the words of those operating these places. They describe their backgrounds and experiences as they seek to support and nurture people doing Christian ministry.

1

SECTION ONE
The Need for Oasis: Why Pastors and Missionaries Burn Out

Jim and Vonnie Healy minister in the *Salmon Harbor Oasis* in Winchester Bay, Oregon, using a yacht to house their ministry guests.

Jim and Vonnie, married in 1975, have been in ministry since 1979. They pastored churches in California and Oregon and led the Northwest Region of the Nazarene Church as Superintendent. Jim holds a Doctor of Ministry

degree from Nazarene Theological Seminary. Jim and Vonnie were trained and certified as Marriage Enrichment Facilitators. They have conducted Marriage Enrichment events in the U.S. and around the world for pastors and missionary couples and enjoy sharing with couples who come to their Oasis.

The Healys are uniquely gifted to love and support pastors and missionaries, with a wide range of experience in pastoral ministry and leadership. Since 1985 they have been helping ministry leaders address various concerns related to conflict resolution, burnout, marriage, family, and other personal issues through encouragement, prayer, and friendship. Jim and Vonnie have served as Life Impact hosts since 2010 and took on the additional role of U.S. and Canada Regional Directors in late 2013.

Jim: We could talk for hours about pastors and burnout. When I was pastoring I was gone all the time, and when you do come home you're exhausted and don't have much time for family. People have such critical needs they just suck you dry, and you don't have much left when you're at home.

Vonnie: I think being a pastor is a 24-hour job, and no one realizes that you have to be on call 24/7 for everyone's crisis. So you're always in crisis mode

LI: *There seems to be a common belief in congregations that pastors don't have these kinds of problems, or if they do, there's something wrong with them. As a result, pastors don't feel free to share their own struggles. Do you see that?*

Jim: That's very much the case. Before they'll want to share with you, you have to be in the "brotherhood of pastors" in order to understand. But we found that even if you're in the same denomination, in the same district, it can still be hard for them to share. But now (in our Oasis work) we're "safe, confidential" caregivers. They come to us and feel they can share freely because we don't have their career in the palm of our hands. We're not reporting back to their leadership. They can be free with us to pour out their hearts, and that's what they do.

Mark and Jayne Brewster minister in the *Shepherd's Rest Oasis* in Lewiston, Idaho.

Mark and Jayne were married in 1978. Since 1984 they have lived in Lewiston, Idaho, where Mark served for thirty years as Senior Pastor of Orchards Community Church until June 2014, when they joined Life Impact full time. Throughout their time in the Lewiston-Clarkston Valley, Mark has had many opportunities to encourage and be encouraged by numerous pastors in the region. Additionally, he has ministered to pastors and church leaders in Asia and Africa.

Mark: In my own experience I did burn out one time, or nearly did. That's when I took my first sabbatical. Then eight years ago I had a heart attack, and when I was in the hospital they said there are no factors apart from stress that would have caused the heart failure. So in 2011 we took another sabbatical, and it was during that time I came to believe there are too many expectations pastors place on themselves, plus those placed on us by our churches. Then there are expectations we as pastors think God has placed on us. That's a heavy "performance burden" to carry as well.

I also believe there are cultural factors influencing how the pastoral role is pursued, which are not consistent with what the Scriptures say. One illustration is that pastors today sense their job is to be the CEO of a business as opposed to being a shepherd of God's flock. Most people I know who go into ministry, don't do it to be a CEO. They go in Christian ministry because God has called them to feed and care for the flock. So there are things out there that create tremendous pressure and stress to move pastors away from their true calling.

I recently had a conversation with a couple of ministers who said, "We're not burned out yet, but we are ready to quit the pastorate." I asked them, "What does the word 'pastor' mean to you?" They replied, "a shepherd." So I said, "Right. In Scripture when Jesus asked Peter 'do you love me?' and Peter said 'yes,' Jesus replied, 'Feed my sheep. Care for my sheep.'" (John 21:16-18) That's not always what people are looking for in a pastor today. And it's not always what a pastor thinks he's supposed to be doing today. But the reality is, if they're not doing that, they're no longer being a shepherd.

I think another factor that plays into this is how easy it is for some, in the busyness of ministry, to try and draw life from the ministry rather than from the Lord Jesus. Ministry is the overflow of the life that is already in us. Often what happens is we start to see ministry as the source of our life rather than the Lord Jesus as the source of our life. That's a dead-end street. In John 15:5, He did say, "Apart from Me, YOU can do nothing!" [Emphasis added]

Harold and Kimmy Otterlei minister in the *Elderberry House Oasis* in West Linn, Oregon.

Harold and Kimmy Otterlei, married since 1983, have been involved in

pastoral care for over twenty-five years. Harold started as a staff pastor and then served as a senior pastor for sixteen years. During this time they raised three children. Fourteen years into their marriage, Harold had a life-threatening brain hemorrhage which changed their lives dramatically. Kimmy became his caregiver as Harold recovered and was rehabilitated.

He made a miraculous recovery but over time came to realize he had some new limitations. Still sensing a call to ministry, he transitioned into hospice chaplaincy. This experience has given them a deep appreciation for those who have serious physical ailments and their caregivers. Harold holds an Masters of Divinity degree. Both of them have given themselves to pastoral care and counseling married couples to help enrich marriages.

Kimmy: God created a kind of Life Impact Oasis for us through close friends after our ministry in a church ended abruptly. At that time we experienced the benefits of having someone come along side us, love us, encourage us, and coach us through that difficult and pivotal time in our life and ministry. We had some bad feelings about leaving and were a bit broken. We were sad to leave the people in the church but had a peace about it, as did the congregation. Yet we needed some time to mend. That's a huge piece in our experience of why we are so committed to see other people stay in a role of service.

Harold: I think the key is having someone you can talk to. I've seen statistics about pastors indicating most pastors feel very alone, and there's no one with whom they can process. They don't feel they can deeply share with their denominational leaders nor with the leadership in their church because they're afraid they'll lose their job. They need a neutral, confidential party they can process with, and that's one of the things Life Impact is able to offer.

Tim and Ericka Harris minister in the *Los Pastos Oasis* in Grecia, Costa Rica.

Having been involved in missions since 1992, Tim and Ericka have seen the journey of preparation, training, and commitment necessary to thrive. Their heart is to fortify those who serve cross-culturally on the "front lines" of God's Great Commission. Front-line workers need rest and care. How wonderful for that desire to be accomplished at a small cost to the worker but in a location surrounded with God's creative beauty.

As a result of his fifteen years in business, Tim's skills include building and managing teams to reach common goals, coaching team members for success, listening, and communicating effectively. He also understands and is committed to the value of a "leveraged" approach to ministry—focusing energy toward front-line missionaries to strengthen them so they have a greater impact in advancing the cause of Christ and His Kingdom.

Ericka has a degree in Psychology and was involved in launching a Stephen Ministry at her local church. Much of their missions involvement has been in Latin American countries. Both are fluent in Spanish and delighted to host Life Impact's Oasis in Costa Rica. They consider this an awesome way to use their gifts and serve together to strengthen those ministering on the front lines of God's Great Commission.

Ericka: We deal mainly with Costa Rican pastors here, and their fundamental needs are the same: the need to connect with spouse, connect with God, connect with their family, feeling extreme pressure to perform, knowing who to please, and not

7

feeling or thinking they have a safe place to share.

For missionaries, the cross-cultural aspect adds a unique element to it. Here are some generalities. They feel very alone. They are far from their family or support systems; so being in a cross-cultural setting they have to build that support again in different ways. They also feel their resources are very limited, whether it relates to finances or time or friendship.

Tim: The cross-cultural or "foreigness" element for the missionary might fan the flames of any of the areas they bring to us. There's also that extra element of not having the resources you have access to within your own culture. For example, it seems a lot harder to get stuff done with the government or to educate your children in the host culture. Everyone in a cross-cultural situation operates with fewer resources. Those who are new in the field have a lot more issues in finding these resources because they don't have the connections they had back home. This leads to strong feelings of inadequacy, frustration, and even anger.

As time goes on another cross-cultural challenge starts revolving around the deaths of family members or friends back home and the inability to get back home for funerals, grieving, or other extended-family matters. This creates a strong feeling of inadequacy and frustration. So we help the missionary determine what they have control over and what they don't. We also help them focus on the One who is in control of all things. This perspective helps eliminate a lot of the frustration and helps them live at peace with major life issues outside one's control arising in the foreign context.

Ericka: We help them recognize which circumstances are changeable and which circumstances they have to find resources to accommodate.

Craig & Karen Hamlow, formerly ministered in the *Alaska Oasis* in Soldotna, Alaska. They now minister with Potter's Inn in Divide, CO

Craig and Karen and family were ministering through a Life Impact Oasis in Soldatna, Alaska, hosting pastors who lived in the Alaskan bush and wilderness areas. Recently, Potter's Inn invited the Hamlows to join their team in Colorado as their gifting, experience in missions, pastoral care, and heart to shepherd the souls of others was so fitting. After serving for nine years in Alaska as caregivers for missionaries and pastors, they now serve the Potter's Inn mission as key ministry and administrative staff in their work of soul care and spiritual transformation.

Craig is overseeing the upkeep and operations of the Aspen Ridge Retreat center while Karen is managing the office and behind-the-scenes operations. Craig is also leading outdoor soul-care adventures with Potter's Inn guests through hiking and camping. When not at Potter's Inn, you'll find the Hamlows fully intertwined with their three children.

Craig: I think the issue that is probably unique to the environment in Alaska is the cold and the dark, especially in the winter months. Many of the pastors out there battle with depression. Normally a warm day in winter is thirty degrees. Usually it's in the teens and even colder. Winter days are short, it doesn't get light until ten, it's dark around four, shadows are always long, and it feels like dusk all the time. That's all there is—dusk. So we find the weather and the light, combined with the isolation, kind of create a perfect storm for pastors to really feel despondent.

The majority of pastors live in the villages, and they live in a fishbowl. It's a tribal culture, and in a village most people are related. Typically there's 10 percent white people in the village, and the rest are native. And everybody knows what the pastor is doing. People might say "I was walkin' by the pastor's house the other day, and I heard somebody shouting. I wonder what's goin' on there?" The pastor might have been yelling at the TV football game. So you just live in that fishbowl. And churches are typically very poorly attended, which creates financial strain.

Before ministering with Life Impact, we worked with Arctic Barnabas ministries. We flew planes back and forth to the pastors. In that context we saw a really high turnover rate among pastors. One pastor lasted for six weeks and quit. He got into the village and realized "Oh no, I've gotten way into the deep end, and I don't know how to swim."

Celeste Allen ministers in The *Oaks Oasis* in Porano, Italy.

Celeste Allen spent nearly twenty years working in the corporate sector and as a freelance editor. During that time she took several summers off to teach English at colleges and universities in Asia. In 2000 Celeste moved into full-time

ministry in the United Kingdom at the International Office of Frontiers, where she organized events and conferences in Europe and Asia. Celeste served as Frontiers' International Member Care Coordinator before joining the staff of Life Impact.

Throughout her career in secular work as well as in full-time Christian work, Celeste has offered hospitality, encouragement, and compassionate listening to cross-cultural workers from around the world. She is trained in inner healing prayer, coaching, biblical counseling, and mentoring. In light of her strengths and training, she offers spiritual formation retreats for small groups as well as personal retreats for individuals and couples. She belongs to a community of believers called the Eschol Community.

Celeste: Back in the 80s I was in my early twenties, going to mission conferences and involved with the mission committee at my church. I began meeting missionaries and saw how tired they were and how much they needed a safe place to chill out, relax, and regroup. I was living in Pittsburgh, Pennsylvania, probing around to see what opportunities there might be for me to have a house where people in missions could come for rest and reflection.

LI: *Celeste went to work for Frontiers, based in England, where she again saw firsthand the needs of people in ministry.*

Celeste: I was executive assistant to the International Director for a couple of years and then the administrator for the Field Office for several years, doing conference planning and that sort of thing. Again I was hosting missionaries in my home, and at work I don't know how many times I had people crying in my office because they were just burned out, had difficulties in the field with teammates, with leaders, whatever. This continued to move my heart.

Amber Stark ministers in The *Good Book Oasis* in Vrbovce, Slovakia.

Amber Stark is an MK (missionary kid) who grew up primarily in England and Canada. At eight years of age she accepted Christ as her personal savior and pledged to use her life for the Lord in whatever way He chose. She attended Trinity International University where she received her degree in Elementary Education. Desiring to minister to other MKs, she worked for two years at an American Christian school in Seoul, South Korea. She has also spent time on mission teams working in Siberia, Russia, and the Philippines.

Amber: I find a lot of missionaries just want someone to talk to who is outside of their ministry. So it's not someone who will undermine their ministry. It's not a member of their team. It's not their boss who might say, "Oh my, you're crazy; you need to go home." I'm totally separate from their "chain-of-command." I'm a safe person to talk to, and most of the time I don't have to initiate the conversation. They just want to talk. They don't want advice. They don't want me to tell them everything's going to be okay. They just want to talk or share their story. I've had people sit down next to me and say, "You know, I've really been struggling with ...," and they just talk.

I've had some people ask me to talk with their kids about being a missionary kid, and I can see the kids are reassured when I tell them, "Oh yeah, I know what that's like. I'm a missionary kid, too." It's nice for them to know what they're going through is normal. It's hard when no one else around you understands, or they think you're very strange. When they talk to me I'm not surprised. You can't surprise me; I've seen it. I'm not a counselor, and I don't pretend to be. I'm just a listening ear.

Missionary kids live with a unique set of circumstances it's difficult to understand unless you've been one. They need to talk to someone who's been in their situation. I see it in their attitudes and outlook on life: not expecting to get holidays, not expecting to have time with their family, not expecting to have close friends, etc. Some families make a specific effort to deal with these things and spend time with their kids, but I knew other missionaries who felt that the mission was more important than that. So they didn't give as much time to their families as they should.

Carlos and Liliana Torres, minister with Life Impact in Patagonia, Argentina.

Carlos and Liliana Torres have had a very successful career in both mission service and the local church pastorate. They started their mission career working with Operation Mobilization (OM) on the Doulos, *the ship that went from port to port bringing literature, biblical teaching, evangelism, and practical help.*

In that capacity they served as team leaders and eventually as a National (Regional) Director for OM Argentina. Later, because of their hearts and gifts, they started providing care services to OM staffers. They still support the OM ministry with both care and translations services.

Presently they live in Esquel, Argentina, where they strengthen missionary and pastor guests coming for care services, while also serving as pastors of a local church.

Carlos: My wife and I have been working with Operation Mobilization, and the last job we developed for them was member care for missionaries in Latin America. So we saw the need to have a place to receive them in a more personal way. We also knew the need from our own experience in ministry, and we saw missionaries going home because they were worn out and felt nobody cared about them, especially in Latin America, which is quite new to the concept of "missionary member care." We have been moving and living in houses we rented or someone lent us, but we have always been available to people in ministry who need help.

At this time we live in a parsonage of a small church here in Esquel, and we don't have a larger place for people to stay. But we always have an extra room ready to receive anyone who would like to come. So we're also very busy with all that goes into church ministry for a pastor—preaching on Sundays, leading music, pastoral counseling, visitation, etc., but never too busy to host pastors or missionaries coming for care.

We look forward to the time when our own place is finished and we can do a better job of care for pastors and missionaries coming our way. At that time we'll continue involvement with our church but not as the pastor.

(They presently have purchased land and will renovate a structure to expand their guest facilities.)

LI: Describe the community in which you live and work as pastor.

Carlos: Esquel is a small town of 40,000 people. We are in the mountains in the southwest part of Argentina near the border with Chile. Our church is a small congregation of about seventy to eighty people who are members. They are a mixture of cultures, including indigenous Indians and people who have European backgrounds. My father came from Spain and my mother from northern Italy. I am Argentine because I was born here, but I am descended from the Latin part of Europe. We have people in the church who don't know how to read or write and people who are professors at the university. It's quite a challenge to preach on Sundays and aim for everyone.

But this experience has sensitized Liliana and me to the needs and issues of pastors as well as missionaries.

SECTION TWO
The Dynamics of Life Impact Care

There are various methods of approach in helping people in ministry cope with the circumstances of their calling, as the following conversations demonstrate.

East patio of the Los Pastos Oasis, Grecia, Costa Rica

Tim and Ericka Harris (Costa Rica)
    We live in a world of rhythm. God gave us the model of that

when He rested on the seventh day of creation. It's important to find the right rhythm where all the components get attention. So ministry gets attention, self-care of your personal relationship with God gets attention, your spouse gets attention, your family gets attention, your fun times get attention; all of those have times when you can get into them.

Some people have different rhythms. They can go for longer periods without certain things getting attention, and yet they're still healthy. People need to find their own rhythm, and we help them discover what that is. Some people need to get a different beat going. It's kind of like being an experienced symphony conductor who's heard the music so many times he knows what it's supposed to sound like. For us it means listening for what's not working when we're talking with someone who's burned out or wondering what to do next. We listen for the parts that aren't working and try to fine tune those.

One hundred percent of this insight into a guest's situation is inspired by the Holy Spirit. We might have some gifts that we use, but the promptings to speak or to not speak, that's a matter of being in tune with God. Often we just point out the rough spots we're hearing in their story and ask them what their thoughts are about what might be working. Occasionally we might give advice, but often they kind of know they need to make some changes and just need a third party to help them talk their way through it. We act like a conductor who wants to hear the song played well.

LI: *It would seem you have to establish a certain sense of safety for people to share at this level. How do you establish that?*

Ericka: We first talk about confidentiality, and we share meals just to establish rapport. Then we listen and ask questions about what they're sharing.

Tim: We have rarely struggled with an Oasis guest not sharing anything. They might not go to the deepest level. They may be at the experience level when they really need to get down to thoughts and feelings. That means we need to keep asking questions and have them ponder because the human mind is an amazing thing: when asked a question, it wants to answer even if it's conflicted and doesn't want to go there.

As far as establishing rapport, people find us and want to come for an Oasis visit. It's not like we're strong-arming people to come here. They're kind of looking for help at this point. They are motivated for some personal reason. If it's a couple or a family, somebody there knows they need it. If our time in sharing together becomes more critical than the coaching or a caregiving relationship, we go get help. Second, we care, and we listen, being interactive and present with them. We listen to what they say, watch their body language; all the different gamuts of it. Most people will give you that kind of active listening for maybe thirty seconds, and we do it for three or four days.

The Shepard's Rest Oasis, Lewiston, Idaho

Mark & Jayne Brewster (Idaho)

One of the things we like about Life Impact's ministry and leadership is they give us room to do what we do. Our ministry is based on relationships we've already established in this broader Washington and Idaho State community. So we have a two-fold kind of strategy where we want to provide rest from the battle but also rest amidst the battle. By that I mean we desire to have pastors and missionaries use our Oasis as a place to come to for retreat from the battle—to use our house for rest and refreshment. We also go out and initiate a coffee time or a lunch time and process with them while they're engaged in some of the stuff they find themselves in. We're very excited about that. Not just kind of, but very excited. That type of caring help keeps them strong for ministry.

The Intrepid, our Salmon Harbor Oasis in Winchester Bay, Oregon

Jim and Vonnie Healy (Oregon)

LI: Describe how you learned to create a safe place—a safe Oasis—for people in ministry.

Jim: Through all the retreats we've done and spending time with people, we've learned that the first thing many of them need is a lot of rest. They stay on our thirty-four-foot boat that's very private and a place where they can get in touch with the Lord. This is critical to their physical and spiritual well-being. Then we can invite them over to our home for fellowship or processing, depending on their needs. We can coach them along and hopefully get them ready to go back into whatever their ministry is. We also pray for their time continually while they stay on our yacht.

LI: Vonnie, you also spend one-on-one time with the folks who come to your Oasis. Tell us about that.

Vonnie: That's true. We especially get the one-on-one time with some of the young couples. The wife will often download to me and share her feelings on all types of issues and topics. It's usually a very intense and heart-felt confidential conversation. Part of the reason we can enter into their lives and pain is we're wounded healers ourselves, and we've been healed through the input of other people. So we understand a lot of their pain and what they've been through.

A lot of what we do is active listening. They need someone to talk to who won't judge them and who can't control their destiny. We try to be "shepherds" who enter into their issues and pain to ask good questions that help them think about their own answers, solutions, and future steps.

The Wold's Oasis, Rapid City, South Dakota

Jim & Carol Wold (South Dakota)

Jim: My background is primarily in counseling. From the get-go, Life Impact wanted all of the staff to have coaching training; so Carol and I did that. As far as our style of work with people goes, we might be doing counseling and coaching and mentoring simultaneously.

Counseling can be defined loosely as "looking back at the past and how that's impacted them, thinking a little more deeply and looking for insight so we can address the issues that have come up in their marriage, ministry, and so on."

Coaching can be defined as "engaging with someone who wants

to move ahead in a certain direction, and we simply ask important, significant, and insightful questions." The coach does not have an agenda to steer the client in a certain direction. They're simply helping the party to process their own thoughts and perspective by asking questions to help them stay motivated and going in the direction that the client has ascertained they want to go in. Mentoring is coming alongside someone to share in their real life experiences. For instance in a sharing session with a couple we might share some experience within our marriage.

In a clinical sense the counselor would not share about their own life. I wouldn't call myself a clinical counselor by any stretch of the imagination, but when we're working with people we share about our own life, experiences, history, and troubles—past, present, and anticipated in the future. And we ask questions and help people move in the direction they aspire to go.

When people come to stay at our Oasis, they can be put off or a little bit intimidated by the word "counseling." We prefer to say we're walking alongside them, being engaged in their life and helping them think through the processes and challenges they're in. There may be some intense periods of counseling, but later in the day we may be playing a table game or going out for a hike, kayaking on a lake in the Black Hills. We just engage with them and relate to them in a whole variety to contexts.

LI: You engage in what is described as "Biblical counseling." Can you describe what that is?

Jim: I received my Masters' degree in Biblical Counseling from Grace Theological Seminary. I believe and practice that the Scriptures are completely sufficient to address the various issues people struggle with. So when I work with people we can talk about anorexia, bulimia, any of those kind of issues. The Scriptures are sufficient to address them. Also, when we deal with any kind of relational or spiritual issue in their life there is so much in the Scriptures to address those kinds of questions. We prefer to deal with life issues based on the truth of God's word because of our conviction concerning the Bible.

And our approach is more than just sharing some Bible verses with them. There's a passage in Jeremiah 2:12-13 that gets to the heart of most of the issues. It says, "'Be appalled at this. O heavens, and shudder with great horror,' declares the Lord. 'My people have committed two sins.'" (You might think, "Just two sins? There are at least ten Commandments!") It continues, "They have forsaken me, the spring of living water, and they've dug their own cisterns, broken cisterns that cannot hold water."

The essence of that profound passage is He's telling the Israelites, "You've turned away from me and looked for something else to satisfy the thirst for me I created you with." Nobody is completely self-sufficient. Anything can be a cistern to try to take the place of God. It can even be one's spouse or one's ministry. Then there are all the vices out there like drugs or materialism; all these kinds of things. When we turn away from the Lord, we're trying to satisfy the God-given longings in our lives through something that cannot do it. When God doesn't come through for us in a way we might expect, people are inclined to look elsewhere. When those things don't bring fruition to what we're pursuing, we may try to numb the pain. Alcohol can numb pain. Ministers may be going a hundred miles an hour doing all kinds of 'ministry for God' to numb pain.

My responsibility before God as I work with people in this care ministry is simply to offer them love and offer them truth. It's not my responsibility to fix anybody or make sure all the pain in their lives goes away. God may be orchestrating it and capitalizing on it for His purpose in their life. It's not my purpose to help people become more self-sufficient because God has a heart for us to be dependent on Him.

Summer at the Elderberry Oasis, West Linn, Oregon

Harold and Kimmy Otterlei (Oregon)
LI: You're helping people grow in their capacity to do ministry, and they're helping you grow in your counseling and coaching. What is the role of asking good questions in these circumstances?
Harold: It's critical. As an example, in hospice work whenever we have a new patient I do a spiritual assessment. We have four standard questions:
What are the things that give you meaning and purpose in your life?
How do you connect with people: friends, co-workers, family?
What do you do to find peace?
What has given you joy and happiness?
I'm always amazed how much those four questions reveal. By the time I've finished talking with people I have a clear idea of what I might be able to do with and for the person.
LI: Those four questions are pretty thoroughly dealt with in Scripture, and most of the people with whom you work are well-versed in Scripture. What sidetracks them?
Harold: I think some become so engrossed in the minutia of life and ministry they can't see the forest for the trees. They lose perspective.
Kimmy: That's why it's important for a Christian worker to come away and withdraw periodically. It's important for them to get out of their present ministry and life situation. If they do that [retreat] on a regular basis, it could change being sidetracked. Once they get lifted up above the minutia, their perspective changes. They see things differently. Often they see things more realistically. That strengthens them, and they move forward more powerfully.

The Alaska Oasis, Soldotna, Alaska

Craig & Karen Hamlow (Alaska)

Pastors who come in from the bush will normally stay for a week. Usually the first day or so is just a lot of sleeping: they just want to rest. After that there's a lot of debriefing. I will often start by asking, "Tell me about your last six months in ministry." You can see the wheels turning, and there's this big deep breath, and then the conversation can go for hours or days. They just don't get debriefing in their village. Who can they talk to? Everyone else in their village is involved in whatever they're trying to talk about.

One of the biggest things I have to do is just debrief. Then as the conversation continues it always turns in to a bit of coaching that goes like this: "How can we go from here, where I see you're exhausted, to a way we can change that? What can we set up that's going to make life different so you can find a different rhythm? You're still going to be tired, but how can you make sure you get the help and rest you need so you can be effective long-term rather than just binge and purge? You don't want to work as long as you can, as hard as you can, until you can't stand it anymore, and you come out of the bush on your last gasp for a breath of fresh air."

The other piece of it is I always ask them, "What are the things that refresh you? Let's see if we can engage in some of those." I had a pastor and pastoral caregiver come up from the lower forty-eight last year, and one of the things that refreshes him is fishing. It was late July or early August, and I went out with him as the salmon fishing was tailing off and the trout were coming up the river to snatch up all those salmon eggs. In the ten days he was here I fished with him at least seven of those. I think he fished every day he was here. He said, "I have never felt better than when I was standing in the river or sitting on a river bank with you and we were talking or just sitting. That refreshed me more than anything has in the last number of years." It wasn't rocket science for me. It was sitting rod-in-hand next to a guy and being available for him.

There have been other guys that just want to take a walk in the woods or sit by a lake or stream; so we do that. Part of the flavor of this Oasis is helping people from the lower forty-eight states learn to use the outdoors as a tool to help them reconnect with God and reconnect with who they are deep inside. These things get covered over with the 'daily-ness' of life.

Long View of the Oaks Oasis, Porano, Italy

Celeste Allen (Italy)

LI: Celeste describes one of the tools she uses to help guests as "compassionate listening." What is that exactly?

Celeste: It's active listening with the heart open to what the Lord might want to say. I'm taking in what people are saying, feeding back to them and then, depending on the context we're in, praying into what they're talking about, being open to the Spirit. Sometimes the Lord might say, "Just keep your mouth shut and hold their hand." It's a matter of keeping hearts and ears open to how the Lord is leading the conversation. I don't have any answers. I ask questions. I pray with people and have them pray. But it's a rare thing that I will give advice. Sometimes we may not know what we have to do, but the Lord knows.

LI: While she doesn't spend a lot of time giving advice, Celeste says there are occasions when her experience comes into play.

Celeste: I had a woman who emailed me on a Saturday and said she was in Italy and wanted to come on Monday if the Oasis was open. It was; so she came. She was really struggling with her team situation: unexpected changes in structure, new people coming onto the field, and she was struggling and feeling estranged from the organization. She was desperately overworked and not really feeling understood by the people she was working with. She just needed to talk, cry, and be heard.

She spent about three days sleeping, watching DVDs, talking, and crying. Then I was able to say "OK, what steps forward can you make here?" We listened to the Lord together about these situations. That's one time when I sensed I should take off my compassionate listening hat and say something directly. I shared some things I felt she shouldn't continue doing, or she would put herself into a very bad situation. She said she'd never thought of her situation in this light. But I encouraged her to give further consideration to her direction. This was helpful to her.

The Good Book Oasis, Vrbovce, Slovakia

Amber Stark (Slovakia)

One family asked me, before they arrived, to talk to their kids. They were from New Zealand and had been living in Austria for fourteen years. They had three children. One thing I asked the kids was "do you feel more New Zealand or Austrian?" Two felt more like New Zealanders, and one felt more Austrian. I said, "It doesn't really matter which one you are. We are all different and unique." We talked about how an MK's identity is difficult to determine by nationality. When I was growing up I wasn't British even though I lived in England. I wasn't American even though that's where I was born. What was I? Just for them to hear from someone else who lived with the same questions—and who told them it was a normal thing to consider—helped raise their spirits and made them feel more normal.

LI: How do you initiate the conversations with children?

Amber: I usually work with the parents first. It's their responsibility. One way I explain this issue to the parents is to say, "Put yourselves in the shoes of your kids. Then consider: If your dad has a job and it keeps him away from you, you can get mad at the job and mad at the boss. But if your dad works for God, then you either get mad at God and you feel guilty, or you want your

27

parents to be more there for you and you feel guilty."

I tell them it's not the kids' responsibility to change their feelings of guilt—they are paralyzed in that. It's the parents' responsibility. I remind the parents their relationship with God comes first; their relationship with their family comes second; and ministry is third, or should be. I just try to help parents keep in mind that their children are their biggest ministry. It can be a delicate issue. I try to do it tactfully. I'm not a confrontational person. I try using examples from my own life to sort of hint to them about the importance of family if I sense their kids are wrestling with issues only the parents can help resolve.

I love families. Family has always been hugely important to me. Helping families find ways to spend time together and grow stronger seems to be a wonderful thing and something I truly enjoy. So my Oasis is geared more toward families. The past two years I've actually done an MK Retreat at The Good Book Oasis which has been hugely successful. Each year the kids want a repeat the next year.

Mountains in Patagonia, Argentina

Carlos & Liliana Torres (Argentina)

LI: Tell us about encounters that illustrate what you do when people in ministry need help.

Carlos: A missionary couple was going through a crisis in their marriage and had started the divorce proceedings. The wife came to us, and we had a week when we talked and listened with her. She finally moved to our town with her daughters, but now she and her husband are going back together. Praise God for that. They have been serving the Lord in Brazil and South Africa, and now they will start a new life in Brazil.

A Uruguayan missionary who used to work in Eastern Europe met us when we were working in Honduras. When she had some conflict with her team on the field she came to us to spend a few days to unburden what she was going through. At the end of that time she returned to the work. She and others in Uruguay know we are always available, but we want to extend our help to a wider mission field as the Lord opens doors.

When we started to develop the member care ministry in Latin America the main concern of the team leaders in each country was our insistence on confidentiality. If a worker would come to us about their leaders, the leaders would want to know everything they said. We said it doesn't work like that. When they come to us we will encourage them to take steps to confront you and deal with the problem and solve it. But we are not going to come straight to you after we talk with the workers and tell you everything they said. This caused the leaders to be concerned that the workers would say bad things about them, and they wouldn't know it and have a chance to defend themselves.

Some workers had trouble with pastors in their church, and it was the same situation. They asked us to please not tell the pastors about their problems because they were afraid of losing support. We try to create a sharing environment where the workers feel safe to share the deep things of their hearts. So reporting back to others is not something we do unless it relates to very serious issues like suicide or abuse.

LI: What keeps you in Argentina?

Carlos: We tried to serve the Lord in other countries. We tried to go to Spain, but doors didn't open. We tried to go to Italy, but the person we talked to there couldn't understand the ministry of member care. He thought it was just patting their backs and telling them good things and then doing nothing. He said Christian workers should concentrate on work and meeting their goals. He couldn't understand that if the workers felt they were understood, they would function in a more effective way in the field.

There's also the issue that many here don't understand the importance of member care. They often have the attitude of the gentleman I mentioned before. But up to now the Lord has kept us in Patagonia. We are from Buenos Aires originally, a big city where there are many Christian activities. We see many people going out from there into the mission field without the kind of personal support they need. So we think maybe this is where we belong. We can help. This is also a nice area with mountains, trees, and lakes. People like to come here from other areas and countries. So we thought maybe we can combine the local pastoral ministry with a hosting ministry. That's why we are still here and waiting upon the Lord for the expansion of the work.

LI: So what's the reward for dealing with all these challenges?

Carlos: To see the church grow with new members coming in and new people getting to know the Lord. Although it's difficult, we are accomplishing a mission here. We have been involved with pastoring churches for over twenty-two years. That's why now our desire would be to concentrate more on hosting, refreshing, and coaching the workers. We'll do both for now—the pastoring and missionary care—until such time as we can totally focus on the care work.

SECTION THREE
How People are Called to This Work

The ways in which people have been called to do this challenging work often demonstrates God's hand in the process.

Tim and Ericka Harris (Costa Rica)

Ericka: Before we got married in 2001 we each knew that missions would be a part of our lives. Our church was sending out a lot of short-term missionaries, and then in 2003 it sent out its first long-term missionary to do a second term in Russia. The missionary confided in me that the team was going through a difficult time, and they needed a team to come out to pray and encourage. Tim and I did that, and God touched our hearts and gave us a vision of what could be if we provided care to missionaries.

But when we returned the church didn't know what to do with us. Through circumstances we moved to a different county in Southern California and joined a church with a care pastor on staff. We shared with him we wanted to care for missionaries, and he understood. He said he would train us and shift us over to the mission ministry. So for six years, while working in this capacity within the church, we tried to keep up with what was going on in missions outside the U.S.

In 2009 we attended the Pastors-to-Missionaries conference in Colorado, an annual meeting for caregivers. Friends of ours at the conference knew of a home purchased for missionary care

31

purposes in Costa Rica, specifically for use by Life Impact. They asked, "How would you like to care for missionaries in Costa Rica?" If we could have picked anywhere in the world to do mission work it would have been in Latin America, and Costa Rica was ideal.

Tim: We had done a lot of missions work in Central and South America, and Ericka is Latina; so I married into a Latin culture. Costa Rica would be ideal. Our friends introduced us to Dave and Sheri Grissen, founders and President of Life Impact. We had dinner together and heard of the Life Impact ministry and the need for someone to go to Costa Rica and develop that house into an Oasis for care.

After that dinner I told Ericka, "I think we could be a good fit for Life Impact, but I'm not sure we're what they're looking for." Behind that comment was the fact that most care organizations were looking for more experienced or retired missionaries and pastors. Several times in interviews we heard, "You're young and don't have a lot of experience." Actually we had experienced a lot of caregiving in short-term missions and our church situation, but we were not crusty, older missionaries.

But later Dave called me to say that younger caregivers were needed by the present younger generation of workers and would also anchor the future of missionary and pastor care. Life Impact wanted various ages of staff. So he asked if we would consider joining Life Impact specifically to open the Costa Rica Oasis.

I was not ready to answer that question. So Dave said to take some time to discern what God wanted for us. A major consideration was whether we wanted to uproot our family (our children were ages four and two) and leave a comfortable life in the U.S. where I'd had a job for fifteen years. Ours wasn't an easy life, but it was a comfortable one.

I really felt God was asking "Do you trust me with everything?" In that moment I had to say "kind of," which really means "no." That rocked my world because I knew in my heart God was totally trustworthy. Yet I could not totally give up either. So I said I'd trust Him if I had more savings, and I named my list. Then I thought, "If I had none of that, would I still trust God?" I wanted to say "yes," but I could tell that in my heart the answer was "not really." I found it very difficult to consider getting out of my secure life's boat as Peter did. Finally I said, "The only way forward is to trust God and take the Costa Rica opportunity." So we stepped through the door and found ourselves in this meaningful care ministry at the Costa Rican Oasis.

Amber Stark (Slovakia)

Amber: I was raised as a missionary kid, and so I have a heart for them. I began my work career as a teacher, but I found I couldn't reach MKs as I wanted to in that context. I wanted to connect on a deeper level with the kids and their parents, but somehow this situation didn't work well for that. I was in Korea at the time, teaching. I left there, came back to the States, and started praying about what to do next.

The Lord spoke to me and said "I want you to open a bed and breakfast for missionaries." I thought that was awfully strange, but then I started doing research into missionary issues. I found out how much burnout is a problem for cross-cultural workers, and there was a real need for missionary care in various settings. So I started looking for a mission that would facilitate me in this direction and finally found Life Impact. My calling fit perfectly with what Dave and Sheri Grissen had established Life Impact to accomplish. So I went through the application process, was accepted, and was sent out to establish The Good Book Oasis in Vrbovce, Slovakia.

LI: You've done work in several countries. How did that come about?

Amber: I went to Russia for five months with a young adult's music and drama ministry team. Then when I was in college I went for my student teaching at a missionary school in Japan. Then I worked for two years in Korea as a teacher at an American Christian school in Seoul.

LI: How did you come to create an Oasis in Slovakia?

Amber: I wanted to do care ministry in Europe. I thought it would be very central for people from Asia, Africa, and Europe to come to. I went for a vision trip, travelled around, and looked at some locations. The choices boiled down to a rural versus city setting and a western or eastern country location.

Doing our due diligence, Dave Grissen and I sent out a number of e-mail surveys to a group of fifty missionaries we knew in Europe, asking for their advice and preferences. Many responses came back but didn't help us much since it was about a 50/50 split on setting and location. Basically they said, "We don't care where it's at; just set up an Oasis, and we'll come."

Fortunately one of those missionaries we surveyed knew a committed Slovak couple and their sister who had immigrated to Canada during the communist years, after a harrowing escape scenario through the barbed wire. They still had some property in Slovakia they wanted used for ministry purposes even though they were living in Canada. We were connected with them.

Dave and I took a survey trip over to Slovakia to see the property and agreed to move forward with it. However, due to complications in-country that deal fell through. Then the Slovak couple and their sister said, "We're sorry that doesn't work. So how about us buying you a house you could use as an Oasis?" After I picked myself up off the floor and realized they were serious, we moved forward.

I did another survey and looked at twenty-some houses. I found one that would work well. This couple and their sister bought it on the basis of my recommendation and some pictures of the place without setting foot in the house themselves! That's how committed they were to seeing this ministry go forward. Who in their right mind says to a person, "Hey, let me buy you a house for a care ministry, sight unseen!" That's commitment, and that's an illustration of how God moves in the hearts of His children to get help and care to His workers.

LI: What's the life and culture like in Slovakia?

Amber: Slovaks are very family oriented. They're very kind, generous people. Some Slovak friends take care of me, and they keep an eye on me. I think I'm their pet American, and they watch out for me. They always know when someone's at my house, and if I'm not there, they'll come and check on who's come into my house. I love the Slovaks. The countryside is gorgeous with lots of rolling hills, forests and streams where I live. Central and Eastern Slovakia are more mountainous.

LI: Where do the people who come to your Oasis come from?

Amber: So far I've had missionaries from over twenty-five different countries come here. There have been more than twenty-three different nationalities. I can't even say I've had a majority of Americans. There have been Canadians, British, Romanian, Hungarian, Irish, Czech, Slovak, Polish, Nepali, Austrian, German, etc. I've had some from as far away as Guatemala, China, and Uganda. I find that it's proportionate to their distance how long they stay. People from the surrounding countries may come for a weekend and come more often. People from far away come for at least a week. I've had a couple of people stay for two weeks. It's all families and couples. I've had a couple of mini retreats with three or four missionary families. They're kind of piled on top of each other in my facility, but they don't mind.

LI: Why do you think people are drawn to your Oasis?

Amber: I think this is because there aren't many places like this around Europe. Outside of "word of mouth," most people find us on the internet, and they're so excited to have a place of retreat to go to they can afford. Missionaries can't afford to go to a hotel, especially if they have kids. This place is geared for missionaries. They know they'll be understood and not judged. They won't be expected to speak at church or share testimony or make the kids sing "Jesus Loves You" in a different language. They're just so glad to have a place where they can just be themselves and not have any expectations put on them.

Celeste Allen (Italy)

Celeste: I was working as the Member Care Coordinator for Frontiers in England. I was getting lots of member care newsletters, and that's how I found out about Life Impact. I met with Dave and Sheri Grissen, and Dave wisely suggested that rather than start a retreat center that would sleep twelve to sixteen people, I should start with a house where I wouldn't have to worry about employing a staff and dealing with the headaches of a larger place.

LI: So you found a house in Italy and put together an Oasis. Has Italy proved to be the environment you hoped it would be to do this work?

Celeste: Yes. People find this place absolutely amazing. It is gorgeous. People who have seen pictures and were stunned are even more stunned when they come here. There's something about the beauty of the place that helps people relax. It's pure God, and people can just soak in it. We're in the countryside. The town of Orvieto is about a twenty-minute drive away. There's a farmhouse about a hundred yards from here, and that's the only house you can see. There's an olive grove across the lane. I'm on a hill, and up the road there's a vineyard. It's fields and woods, and it's just glorious. The Italian culture has an in-grained sense of beauty, and it's much more relaxed. Visitors enjoy that, too.

David and Theresa Knauss, Life Impact President (Oregon)

David: We met Dave and Sheri Grissen when they were organizing a mission team for Central Asia. The iron curtain had just rusted out, and Central Asia was wide open for Christian help. At that time we had an interest in going to Kazakhstan. So Dave and I did a survey trip in 1992. We visited Kazakhstan, Moscow, and Poland together, and subsequently Theresa and I joined with the Navigators for this team. Dave became our supervisor and trainer as we prepared to leave for Kazakhstan. We were in Kazakhstan from 1993 to 2007. Dave was our supervisor for the first half of that. Then we switched to another missions agency where we led a church planting initiative as well as accomplished many humanitarian and business projects. In 2009 we took a sabbatical, and Dave became my sabbatical coach, meeting weekly together via Skype or phone.

Theresa: Toward the end of that sabbatical time Dave said, "We'd like you to come and work with Life Impact." Since we had known Dave and Sherri for a long time and felt close to them, and since we also felt a passion for supporting missionaries and pastors after seeing many needs over our fourteen years on the field, we joined Life Impact in 2010.

LI: What led you to Kazakhstan?

David: Theresa had a strong calling for serving the nations. So ever since we met we set our hearts toward finding out where God would have us serve overseas. When we got to Kazakhstan the Soviet Union had just collapsed, and there was a great need for everything from humanitarian aid to English teachers. But our main focus was to church plant and to see the Gospel spread in a formerly Muslim nation under Communist rule. They were trying to transition back to being an independent nation and find out who they were and where they wanted to be. It was a great time to be there and introduce Jesus to them. So we joined the church planting team Dave Grissen and The Navigators were putting together.

Theresa: The first year we were students learning language and culture. Then David became an English teacher for about five years. The remaining nine or so years we worked with humanitarian aid and development. We also worked with medical teams and orphanages. We saw many Kazakhs come to know Jesus as their Lord and Savior and then had the privilege to disciple them through the translated Gospel in their own language. It was a fabulous time—not easy but very rewarding.

We had the privilege to be in the cadre of workers after 1990 that helped plant the national church among these unreached peoples. (The Russian Orthodox and Baptist Churches were there before us but hadn't really penetrated among the national peoples.) Recently we've visited some of the children of the first converts— and many are committed second-generation believers, reaching out in their own lands. This is just as Jesus said, "The gates of hell will not prevail against the church!" (Matthew 16:18)

David: We were privileged to see two churches start, and we supported nationals who started three or four more churches—real multiplication of the Gospel. Our last years there we focused more on caring for pastors. We felt very supported by our leadership since Dave and his care team would visit us in our situation at least once a year. This also showed us the value of caring for Christian workers out in the trenches doing the work.

LI: We're hearing many in the mission field speak of the lack of personal support and counsel they get from their sending organizations. Either it isn't provided or they're reluctant to share with their supervisors the fact that they're struggling.

David: We hear that all the time, and we understand and see the great need for objective caregivers to walk with missionaries in their shoes and hear their needs.

Theresa: David and I are different type of staff from most of those you're talking to at Life Impact because at this time we do not have an Oasis where we can host people. At this point there is no dedicated Oasis in Central Oregon even though this is our headquarters for the organization. We may have that at some point in the future, but our role at this time is to lend support and encouragement to the Life Impact staff themselves. Our job is to care for the caregivers. That's what we came on board with Life Impact to do.

In that context, we've made some visits to our Oases in the field. I've been to Slovakia and some of the U.S.A. Oases. David has been to Costa Rica as well as two Oases under the publicity radar because of their location.

Also, for two years I've been meeting one-on-one via Skype with some of the staff women overseas, and we do a regular Bible study via Skype as well. Our other opportunities are to help missionaries find a place to stay in Central Oregon when they come here for personal help. They can be here for several weeks or several months. We have the opportunity to meet with them, and we've had some really incredible discussions with missionaries through that venue.

David: As we mentioned, in 2010 we came to Central Oregon to support the Grissens in their leadership of Life Impact. In 2012 we were appointed as International Regional Directors. That made our job one of caring for those operating Oases around the world, stimulating their spiritual lives, encouraging them in their work, and ensuring they stayed strong to provide care for others.

Then in the fall of 2014 esophageal cancer was discovered in Dave's chest, and a slow-growing lymphoma was discovered in Sheri's body. Their medical treatments of radiation and chemo became a priority for their lives, putting stress on them with their responsibility of the day-to-day operations of Life Impact. We agreed to become the Interim President of Life Impact, taking the details off their plates and giving them the space for treatment and healing.

They had sensed the Lord wanted them to step down from overall leadership at the end of 2015. So they and the Board were heading in that direction by establishing a president search committee to find someone to follow them. But now in light of this health reality, all of us agreed the presidential search process should start immediately.

Since we had led a non-profit organization for years and were already integrally involved in Life Impact ministry and with LI staff, we decided to apply for the president position. Over a period of several months in the process we met with individual Board members and the search committee. In March of 2015 the Board asked Theresa and me to take over the presidential leadership of Life Impact from the Grissens.

LI: From your experience and perspective, is spreading the Gospel around the world becoming more difficult or less so?

David: I think the difficulty just continues over the years. You have the political issues that happen depending on who's in power. Technology is a plus in terms of reaching certain places now. Now there seem to be more missionaries who are facing crises where they're either being held hostage or they're seeing bloodshed in their family or the neighborhood where there's been shooting, those types of things—some kind of trauma. It seems there's been an increase of that in recent years. So there's more of an incidence of crisis trauma. It adds to the normal cultural struggles, family, organizational, and cultural issues, those types of things.

LI: Just the "normal" cultural barriers would seem to be challenging enough without all the trauma stuff on top of it.

David: That's exactly right. Every culture has its unique barriers and bridges to the Gospel. When we were in the Muslim community one of the greatest barriers that we faced was the sense of honoring their parents and grandparents. They could embrace Jesus and agree with Him and who He was, but to shift from being a Muslim to being a Christian was unthinkable because of the shame, disgrace, and dishonoring of your parents that would be.

LI: Looking forward, what do you see for Life Impact?

David: The whole network of care for missionaries and pastors is growing. Thirty years ago it wasn't even talked about and didn't exist. Twenty years ago it started to gain some interest. Since Life Impact has come into full bloom it has really spread, and now there are conferences in their first or second year globally that are addressing member care issues and trying to pull together member care places and retreats.

Across Christendom member care is really starting to take root.

People are now coming to us saying they've always had this interest and passion, and they've never known how to make it happen. We're providing a platform for that, and they want to know how they can get connected.

LI: Despite all the pressures, people we talk to who are sharing the Gospel in difficult situations seem to be generally happy about their work.

David: We shouldn't be surprised about that because when you're in those situations where your real purpose for being there may be discovered and you could be deported, you are more dependent on the Lord, and so you walk closely with Him. I think we forget that when we work hard to make everything comfortable, we may not be quite as grateful or depending on the Lord as much as we could be.

Harold and Kimmy Otterlie (Oregon)

Harold: I've been in Lake Oswego for six years, and we pastored in Boston for nine years. While we were in Boston we got word that our senior pastor was getting a divorce. It was a classic situation: he later married the church secretary. The pastor and his wife were our role models; so it was awful. We had some 600 people attending the church when this happened. Many people left, and the church doesn't exist today. It broke our hearts, and I often wondered if they could have salvaged their marriage if they'd had help.

We decided to move away, and then I heard about a guy who had been a pastor who was doing a ministry of caring for pastors. They reached out to us and brought us to their home, spent the day with us, talked us through things, and at the end of the day we had this sense of getting a word from God that we were called for such a time as this, as Esther was in Scripture. (Esther 4:14) Having that day when we were about ready to throw in the towel led us to say when we left the house that we were going to work through this. We could have received great value from Life Impact at that time.

Brad & Glaucia Meyer (Brazil)

Brad: Eight years ago my wife Glaucia and I came together in a calling to serve front-line Christian workers, primarily pastors and missionaries, in a home-based, full-time capacity in Brazil. Since that time we have taken three survey trips to Brazil, given up our jobs, sold our home in the St. Louis area, and moved to Brazil to set up an Oasis. At this point in our journey we are renting a small apartment and continuing our search for a larger, suitable place. We continually receive affirmation that missionary and pastor care is a critical need in the country.

Craig & Karen Hamlow (Alaska)

LI: What was your introduction to ministry, and what formed your path?

Craig: Back in the late 80s through the early 90s I attended a Bible college in Iowa and got a degree in biblical studies, having no idea what I would do with it. I just felt that was what the Lord was moving me to. So I thought, "I'll trust Him and see where He takes me." Out of that I got involved in youth ministry for eight or nine years, and in the midst of that I felt God was directing me to pursue missionary aviation. It was undeniable that was where the Lord was taking me. So I took a little step of faith.

Moody Bible Institute had an aviation missionary training program. Typically they don't take anyone over the age of thirty, and I would be thirty when I started, but they let me in. So I said, "Okay, Lord, I don't have the money to do this but I'm going to trust you." We moved from Seattle to Tennessee with $250 in our account. I was able to take $50,000 worth of aviation education, and we came out with a positive balance in our account. God confirmed steps all along the way.

Then we got connected with a person who was just starting a ministry up in Alaska called Arctic Barnabas Ministries. It's a pastor care organization. Barnabas Ministries cares for pastors worldwide, and Arctic Barnabas Ministries focuses on Alaska. We were part of Arctic Barnabas for eight years, doing a mix of hosting pastors here as well as traveling out to visit pastors in the bush. I used my flying and maintenance skills to visit them and maintain the plane the organization owns.

I'd been working in ministry for almost eighteen years when I just needed a break. So we took a sabbatical. It was a great experience to step back and listen to God. I realized that some of the strain and drain I was experiencing was because at Arctic Barnabas we'd gone through a leadership change, and I didn't see eye-to-eye with the new leadership. I decided to go back and give it one more year, and a year later we joined Life Impact.

Some of the reasons were practical, and some were philosophical. The work I'd been doing was more project oriented, and I wanted to get into people's lives and find out how we can help them be more effective in what they do by clearing some of the junk in their lives out of the way. Life Impact was a perfect fit. We already had relationships with many of the pastors out in the bush villages, and we had a home in which we'd already created some hospitality space. So instead of going to them, often they just came to us. That meant I could spend less time travelling and have more time at home with my wife and children.

LI: How did you decide on Alaska for your work?

Craig: Some by default and some by direction. My wife has a blood condition that suppresses her immune system. Most missionary pilots end up in a jungle somewhere: Indonesia, South America, or Asia. We had to cross all those places off our list because diseases like malaria can be serious illnesses, but for Karen they could be fatal. So we had to look stateside where aviation mission work is being done in southern Arizona, southern Florida, or Alaska. And we had to decide hot or cold, and both of us would prefer cold. At the time, Arctic Barnabas was looking for someone with aviation experience and ministry experience, which is a weird combination. So we ended up living and working in the cold climate of Alaska.

Jim and Carol Wold (South Dakota)

Carol: After Jim graduated from Multnomah in 1999 with his Master of Divinity degree, we were looking at church positions. We were also counseling a married couple, and the husband was a part-time staff person at a church. It occurred to Jim there are lots of men out there who could fulfill the church position we were looking at.

Jim: I began to think, "Who's doing ministry to the ministry leaders, to come alongside and help them work through marital issues, burnout, and depression, whatever?" Counseling was my background for quite a few years. So we contacted some people we'd come to know with Barnabas Ministries and got hooked up with them. Barnabas does work similar to that of Life Impact, except they don't host people at their homes.

We had wanted the kind of setup where people could come and stay with us. We met a couple that was considering setting up a ranch-type setting with multiple cottages for people to come and stay for encouragement, counsel, and respite. But then he said the Lord told him to let the vision die. So that left us hanging out there.

Within a few weeks we became aware of Life Impact through a pastor friend who knew Dave and Sheri Grissen. He received a letter from them asking for prayers that another couple would become interested in establishing an Oasis. So we connected with the Grissens and worked together to get an Oasis set up in the Black Hills of South Dakota.

Jim and Vonnie Healy (Oregon)

LI: What in your experience led you to work in the area of supporting pastors and missionaries?

Jim: Before we went to seminary we were laypeople in the church and got into marriage enrichment. After a few years in the pastorate we became involved in marriage enrichment events for laypeople in our district. Then we began to do these programs for pastors and saw the strategic value of helping them in their marriages. If they could have healthy marriages, they could have a healthy church. So we began doing marriage enrichment just for pastors.

Then we began doing it for missionaries as well, and our denomination called us overseas several times to conduct marriage enrichment retreats and care for missionaries through couple-to-couple times. We got very excited about helping pastors and missionaries with their marriages and through pastoral care. Then we retired from the pastoral ministry and now do this care ministry full time.

LI: What got you interested in Life Impact and the Oasis program in terms of helping you do your work?

Vonnie: When we retired we both felt we wanted to start a retreat center for missionaries. So we wrote up our mission statement and our vision, and we were going ahead with it. We live in a beautiful fishing village on the Oregon coast, and we felt that would be a good environment. We went to a Pastors-to-Missionaries conference in Colorado five years ago. There "by chance" we met the Grissens, and when they shared with us about Life Impact's care ministry in hosted Oases, we knew that fit perfectly with what was on our hearts to do.

Jim: It was exactly in line with our personal mission statement and goals. We figured they've already got it going; why reinvent the wheel? So we signed on with them and the Life Impact staff family.

LI: Have they provided you with any tools and processes that are helpful in your work?

Jim: Mainly we got training in coaching. And they helped us with our budgeting and fundraising. Whatever we needed help with they came alongside. And they provided all kinds of encouragement. You can't say enough about our leadership and the LI Staff. They all love the Lord, they love people, and they are really good listeners.

Vonnie: We'd had a lot of training, but what Dave and Sheri Grissen provided specifically was a framework, including the financial part of ministry. They had it all together so we could just fit right in to the Life Impact program.

Mark and Jayne Brewster (Idaho)

Mark: We've been here in Lewiston for thirty years, and I've been the senior pastor at a church of about 300 people. Throughout these years one of the things that's happened is we've had a lot of opportunities to interact with a multitude of pastors and pastoral couples. They have sought me out over the years to talk with me and process things. We were especially impacted by a couple in Boise, where he was pastoring but then resigned eighteen years ago to develop Idaho Mountain Ministries. In the past few years we wondered if this is the kind of ministry we should consider. In 2013 we sought out the Mountain Ministry folks regarding our thinking about this, and they strongly encouraged us. At first we thought we might start our own non-profit, but the more we looked into that direction, the less I liked the idea. Then one night I came across the Life Impact website, and I contacted Dave Grissen about joining Life Impact.

Jayne: My family had provided a place for ministers to come and stay in Washington State, so that was already in my mind, and Life Impact seemed like a good fit for us to do that kind of ministry.

Mark: I already have a lot of interaction with pastors. So I'm continuing on with that. After our experience in ministry, we feel we have something more to contribute that would encourage pastors and ultimately their churches. So we stepped through the door.

AFTERWORD
The Origin of Life Impact
by David Grissen
President Emeritus and Founder, Life Impact Ministries

Dave and Sheri Grissen in Bend, Oregon

Our oldest daughter, Renee, was four years old, and our oldest son, Troy, was two years old when in 1974 we disembarked from a United Airlines plane at Schwechat Airport in Austria. They carrying their security blankets and we our briefcases and documents, all of us breezed through customs without a hitch, to be met by co-workers and ushered to an apartment they had rented for us in the 18th District of Vienna. Our initiation to the City of Music and Austrian *"Gemütlichkeit"* (very comfortable and delightful ambiance) was wonderful. Our idealism was at an all-time high— we were going to change the world for the better while working behind the Iron Curtain, bringing the Gospel, and training Christian leaders.

After our first year of language study and a couple of trips behind the Iron Curtain, our idealism had turned to pessimism. At times I wondered in my heart-of-hearts if I could really "cut" this ministry. As our transition wore on, however, we did get adjusted. We figured out ways to operate that made us seem effective, at least in our own eyes. Another baby came, daily life challenges were handled, we learned enough German to get around the city, and it started feeling like home.

And the believers we met in the communist countries were refreshing and deeply spiritual. Persecution had stripped them of all diversions in life. Higher education was limited. Getting ahead in the system was eliminated. Finding a job that could make a believer a millionaire was non-existent. All these believers had was Jesus. And to Jesus they gave their allegiance, their energies, their time, their adoration, and the focus of their lives. And with that came a dynamic faith, vibrancy in life, and a human spirit that could not be repressed when a dictator said to bow the knee to the state and forget God.

Meeting these precious disciples and doing Kingdom work with them is what got us through the hard times of adjustment, self-doubt, questionings, and despair for fourteen years of ministry behind the Iron Curtain.

After four years of regular travel through the communist borders to build ministry teams of young committed followers of Christ, we had our first home leave, called a "furlough" in our day. We were back in the homeland for an eight-month visit. A supporting church of ours in Zeeland, Michigan provided a "missionary home" for us.

We settled in to do the things international workers do on furloughs: put the kids in a new school and support them through all of their transitions; speak in churches every weekend, meeting throngs of new people; present mission programs in Sunday School classes with our kids; visit individual donors to say "thanks;" make new friends; raise new donor support; buy things you can't find overseas; spend time with the mission org home office for debriefing and business; and in between all of that visit with parents and other relatives. Whew! Where's the rest?

And here's the kicker: I felt that I had personally adjusted to life and the ministry in Europe and was doing great. I was optimistic about our time back in the U.S.A. Things were falling into place, and it would be wonderful to get back and enjoy America. But after our bags were unpacked in the mission house. After our kids were settled in their new schools. After we had said "hello" to most of the family, at least by telephone. Then I discovered, to my chagrin, I did not have the motivation or energy to do anything! I didn't want to call friends. I didn't want to speak in another church. I didn't want to tell another person a story from our ministry. I was exhausted, and I hadn't realized it! That personal spiritual, emotional, and physical condition totally caught me by surprise.

Fortunately I was able to limp along—I really had no choice. Certain things had to be done. But I was also able to change the pace and gain emotional and physical energy again. It turned out to be a good furlough for all of us, and through it the Lord laid the foundation for us to help found another ministry in Eastern Europe called BEE—Biblical Education by Extension. We went back and kept traveling, developing Christian leaders, and leading a team that impacted all of the eight countries of Eastern Europe and the Soviet Union as well. (In fact many of these leaders continue to impact the former Soviet Union and beyond—another story for another day!)

But this type of personal experience of our own humanity, frailties, weaknesses, and inability sometimes to "tough it out," along with other experiences in our many years of mission work, convinced us that times of rest for weary workers were essential for long-term effectiveness.

Was it any accident that in the midst of busy ministry with His disciples, Jesus said to them, "Come with me by yourselves to a quiet place and get some rest"? (Mark 6:31b)

Over the years in Vienna three more children were born into our family, and two others died before taking a breath. We returned permanently to the U.S.A. in 1988 and launched our four oldest into their life tracks. The Iron Curtain rusted out, and new mission opportunities opened up. We re-entered the fray and started building mission teams to penetrate into the Muslim peoples of Central Asia. In 1996 we moved to Tashkent, Uzbekistan with our youngest son, Tony, who was twelve years old.

During our twelve years of ministry in Central Asia, we would periodically come back to the U.S.A. for a couple of months to visit our children and do mission business. Each time back we rented a large house in Sunriver, Oregon for a week where all of our kids, with their spouses and children, would come and join us. These were great times of family reunion and maintaining family unity. And everyone loved Sunriver!

At one of those reunions Sheri and I were walking on a paved bike trail, talking about our future. We both agreed that providing a PLACE of rest and renewal for weary missionaries was something we wanted to do. We wanted to pass on to them the lessons we learned, the good, the bad, and the ugly. We wanted to see them strengthened for the work God had called them to do. So we committed ourselves to do that in our retirement years.

From our first trip into Kazakhstan in 1990 throughout those next twelve years, we saw the Lord plant expat workers teamed up with "…-stan" nationals in five of the unreached peoples of Central Asia. Our time ended. Leadership was transferred to younger workers. So in 2002 we came back to the U.S.A. for our first sabbatical.

One of our sabbatical objectives was to determine our next ministry assignment. Of several possibilities we considered, the thought of establishing a mission oasis for weary harvest workers kept coming to the forefront of our minds, hearts, and prayers. As the sabbatical ended the Lord gave us freedom to "go for it." Counsel of trusted friends and ministry leaders had given us ideas of how to do that. So in March of 2003 we packed up our stuff in Oregon City, Oregon and headed over the mountain to a rented home in Sunriver, Oregon to see if the Lord would bless the commitment to provide care for His workers.

Our thirty-one-year mission career to that point had been with The Navigators, a large interdenominational organization started in the military in the 1930s by Dawson Trotman. Over the years we developed many missionary friendships within The Navigators but had a multitude of missionary friends from other organizations and churches as well. All of them needed care. So instead of taking on a Navigator identify in our new care ministry, we opted for a neutral name and created Life Impact, Inc. in 2003, hoping to minister to harvest workers from many denominations, churches, and mission organizations.

Applying to the IRS for our 501(c)(3) status produced a miracle of encouragement. Normally the process takes several months or longer with letter exchanges between the applicant and the IRS. However, within thirty days our legal and official approval was back with the statement, "If you do what you say you will do, you are approved." Even the IRS was eager to see missionary care houses come into existence! Did the Lord place a Christian in the position of acting on our application?

Missionaries started coming to our rented home in Sunriver. We did what we could to strengthen them and send them back—coaching, mentoring, counseling, processing, and pastoral care.

Then in 2004 the Lord provided a home we purchased that became the stable and official start of Life Impact Ministries. Weary warriors came from the *barrios* of Venezuela, the huge cities of China, the rural areas of Mongolia, the bush of Africa, and also the towns of America.

They represented the ministries of church planting, evangelism, Bible translation, theological education, Christian school teaching, pastoral care, personal discipling, and orphan care. They came for rest, retreat, refreshment, and refocus. They reconnected with the Lord and their spouse and were off, back to their fields to impact the nations!

The Board of Life Impact was operating as a team for Sheri and me. They saw how the Lord was propelling this ministry forward. So in 2006 they said, "Is Life Impact a ministry that stops with Dave and Sheri, or is your vision that it should go beyond you?"

Our hope had been that we could start it, and others would take on the mantle as well. Our world was becoming more dangerous than when we traveled across communist borders and had KGB run-ins. Terrorism was on the rise. Diseases not known to man before were ravaging populations. Cholera was breaking out in more places. The bottom line of all this was: mission and humanitarian aid work was getting more and more stressful. Care would be needed beyond our tenure. So our answer was, "We want Life Impact to go beyond us."

Newsletters went out to ask people to pray for others to join us and help provide care to Christian workers. Within two weeks Jim and Carol Wold connected with us. The Lord laid on their heart some years ago to have a house in which to minister to workers. Jim has counseling training, and together he and Carol helped pastors needing care over the years. Together we were able to establish the Black Hills Oasis in Rapid City, South Dakota, which they still host but now under the auspices of another ministry.

Then came Amber Stark, a missionary kid who wanted to set up an Oasis for missionary kids. She hosts missionary families in Vrbovce, Slovakia. Harold and Kimmy Otterlei connected with us to set up a center in West Linn, Oregon. Celeste Allen connected next. The Lord had laid the vision of missionary care on her heart over 15 years before she met Life Impact. She set up and now hosts a very effective Oasis in Porano, Italy.

And this process goes on, and the Oases go up—around our globe. Costa Rica, Brazil, Argentina, South Africa, Asia, the Middle East, Idaho. Many who have the vision of providing missionary and pastor care in and through a dedicated PLACE are finding us. And we discover that the Lord of the harvest has placed this vision of care on their hearts previously and is now moving them to implement it at this time. Life Impact is one instrument in the Lord's hand to facilitate them into this calling.

Thanks for Joining Arms with Us in This Caregiving Adventure!

That's how we started and a present glimpse of where we are in 2015. We thank you for your support of any of our caregiving staff and the organization. Without you joining us in the saddle, we could not provide these care services to so many around the world. Through your encouragement, prayers, and financial support, you are literally having a broad impact in Kingdom expansion around the globe.

How? Together we are strengthening missionaries and pastors for their ministries in many global locations. If just one worker leaves their place of ministry early for preventable reasons, there is a personal, experiential, and financial cost to the Great Commission enterprise. The financial loss alone could be over $250,000. So you are partnering with us to stem the tide.

ABOUT THE AUTHOR

Michael Beeson has been doing media work for nearly fifty years. His experience includes ten years with CBS radio in San Francisco, where he served in various positions, including News Director and Public Affairs Director. He also hosted many broadcast discussions with movers and shakers in the community and the world.

Mike also did a stint as a newspaper editor and served as Communications Manager for a major Presbyterian church in Seattle. He continues to produce informational material for his church and various community service organizations in Central Oregon. When he's not writing or interviewing people, he produces artwork which has been sold in galleries in Oregon, California, and Hawaii.

While living in Hawaii, Mike and his wife Gail ran a B&B, hosting guests from around the world. When they met the Grissens in Sunriver in 2003 they immediately saw the value of Life Impact's mission of care for Christian workers. They have been strong supporters of this ministry since that time.

Mike and Gail are active in their community and continue to seek the Lord's will in directing their efforts.

Life Impact thanks Mike for writing our story